First Field Trips

State
Capitol

by Rebecca Pettiford

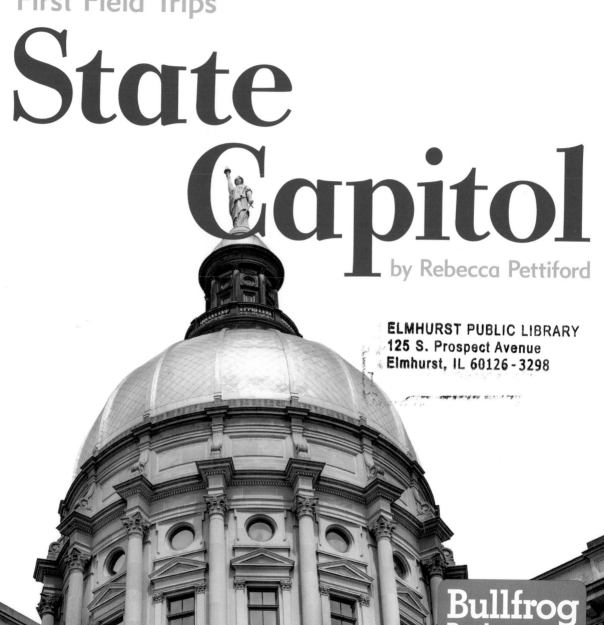

Bullfrog
Books

Ideas for Parents and Teachers

Bullfrog Books let children practice reading informational text at the earliest reading levels. Repetition, familiar words, and photo labels support early readers.

Before Reading

• Discuss the cover photo. What does it tell them?

• Look at the picture glossary together. Read and discuss the words.

Read the Book

• "Walk" through the book and look at the photos. Let the child ask questions. Point out the photo labels.

• Read the book to the child, or have him or her read independently.

After Reading

• Prompt the child to think more. Ask: What laws would you like to see passed at the state capitol?

Bullfrog Books are published by Jump!
5357 Penn Avenue South
Minneapolis, MN 55419
www.jumplibrary.com

Library of Congress Cataloging-in-Publication Data

Names: Pettiford, Rebecca, author.
Title: State capitol / by Rebecca Pettiford.
Description: Minneapolis, Minn.: Jump!, Inc., 2016. |
Series: First field trips | Includes index.
Identifiers: LCCN 2015033990 |
ISBN 9781620312971 (hardcover: alk. paper) |
ISBN 9781624963636 (ebook)
Subjects: LCSH: U.S. States—Capital and capitol—
Juvenile literature. | U.S. States—Politics and
government—Juvenile literature.
Classification: LCC JK1651.A1 P47 2016 |
DDC 320.473—dc23
LC record available at http://lccn.loc.gov/2015033990

Editor: Jenny Fretland VanVoorst
Series Designer: Ellen Huber
Book Designer: Lindaanne Donohoe
Photo Researcher: Lindaanne Donohoe

Photo Credits: All photos by Shutterstock except:
Alamy, 6–7; Corbis, 12–13, 14–15, 18–19; iStock, 3, 4,
20–21, 24; Nagel Photography/Shutterstock.com, 10,
22tl, 22tr, 22bl, 22br; Thinkstock, 1, 16.

Printed in the United States of America at
Corporate Graphics in North Mankato, Minnesota.

Table of Contents

A Day at the Capitol

Our class is on a field trip.

We are at the state capitol.

Who works here?

People in government.

They work for our state.

They work for us!

dome

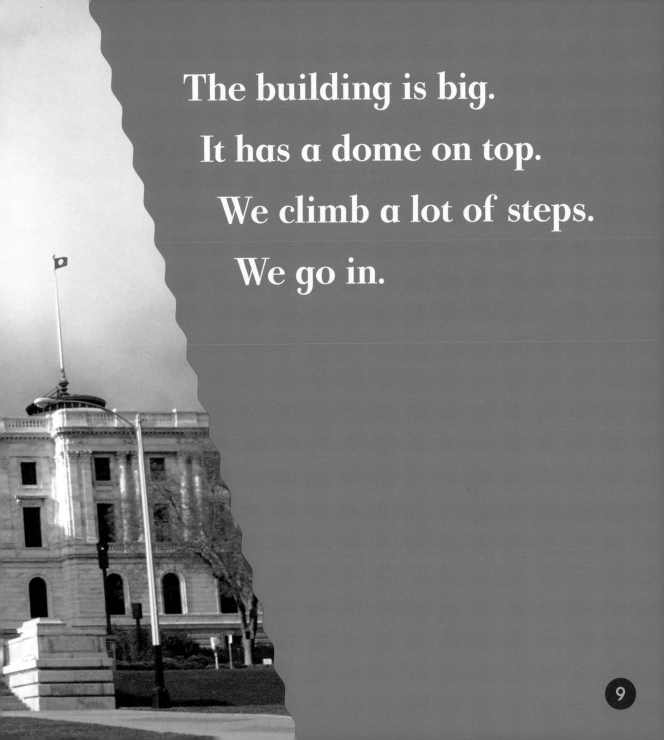

The building is big.
It has a dome on top.
We climb a lot of steps.
We go in.

Wow! It is beautiful.

The floor shines.

We see art.

Look up.

It's the dome!

House members work here.

13

Senate members work here.

What do these groups do?

They pass laws.

Some laws keep us safe.

Others help people work.

We meet the governor.
She is the head of state.

Time to go!

We learned a lot at the capitol.

Inside the State Capitol

dome

House room

Senate room

governor's office

Picture Glossary

field trip
A trip students take to learn about something.

laws
Rules made by a government.

government
The group of people who make decisions for a state or country.

state capitol
The building where a state runs its government.

Index

To Learn More

Learning more is as easy as 1, 2, 3.

1) Go to www.factsurfer.com

2) Enter "statecapitol" into the search box.

3) Click the "Surf" button to see a list of websites.

With factsurfer.com, finding more information is just a click away.